BONSAI

Cultivating, Shaping & Growing

LOG JOURNAL

Jayme | Books
DESIGN

A BIG THANK YOU FOR SUPPORTING INDEPENDANT PUBLISHING
WE HOPE YOU ARE HAPPY WITH YOUR PURCHASE

Why not Subscribe to our once a month newsletter
We promise it to be spam free and contain only fun and informative
news and updates on all our latest release and Editor monthly
recommendations.

SIMPLY SCAN THE QR CODE BELOW

REVIEWS ARE IMPORTANT! ★ ★ ★ ★ ★

Your feedback and comments are greatly appreciated
on Facebook and Amazon. Both help us bring the best to you
and our customers. A few seconds of your valuable time would mean
a huge difference to helping us maintain quality standards
Thank you!

WHY NOT FIND, FOLLOW AND LIKE US ON FACEBOOK!
Comments, question and reviews are always welcome

TIPS FOR BONSAI CARE AND MAINTENANCE

There are four very important things in bonsai care: Watering, Proper soil, Fertilizing, and Positioning and Placement.

PLACING AND POSITIONING

Determining where to place your tree depends on the following factors: Whether your tree is an indoor or outdoor bonsai, what type of tree you have and what its characteristics are the climate, time of year, and other environmental elements. Research on your tree species is highly recommended. The most popular indoor bonsai are the ficus and jade varieties. Temperate bonsai, whether deciduous or evergreen, do better outdoors—so keep them in a garden or on a balcony.

WATERING

Watering is one of the most important parts of ensuring optimal health and growth. Several factors needs to be taken into account when figuring out how regular you need to water: size of the tree, size of the pot, soil type, species, time of year and climate. Only water your tree when the soil starts to get slightly dry. Don't water the tree when the soil is wet, but don't let the soil dry out completely. To easily check whether the soil is moist, push your finger about a centimeter down into the soil—or if you have a moisture meter, that will work too. Never water on a routine. Check each tree individually until you have established what you are doing.

SOIL MIXTURES & FERTILIZING

Choosing the right soil for your bonsai is crucial. Having the wrong soil type can have a dramatic effect on your bonsai health and vigor. The ideal soil type will have to supply nutrients to the tree, have good drainage while retaining water, and supply good aeration. Buying ready-mixed soil from your local bonsai shop or online seems to be the easiest method—but doing it yourself will not only save you money, but you can manage and adjust your soil mixes to the tree species. Bonsai plants and trees require more regular feeding than most houseplants and ornamental plants. Regular fertilizing will keep bonsai small and prevent them from developing spindly limbs. But do not feed sick trees. Let the tree recuperate first before feeding it. As a general rule, feed only healthy trees.

Deciduous should be fertilized weekly during the growing season. Feeding should be stopped once its leaves have fallen. During the fall and winter seasons, give your bonsai a 0-10-0 fertilizer. **Conifer** should be fertilized weekly during its growing season. You must fertilize this a few times during the winter time. During the fall and winter months, you must feed your bonsai tree a 0-10-0 fertilizer. **Tropical and Subtropical** should be fed at least weekly during its growing season. Tropical and subtropical trees will continue to grow all throughout the year and therefore should be fed monthly from fall to springtime.

BONSAI TYPE: _____   **DATE:** _____

PLACING AND POSITIONING

Duration: Visible effect on Bonsai health/condition:

Reactions: Affecting Factors:

WATERING

Frequency:

Visible effect on Bonsai health/condition:

Affecting Factors:

SOIL MIXTURES

Composite:

Estimated quality:

Visible effect/ reactions on Bonsai health/condition:

FERTILIZING

Frequency:

Visible effect on Bonsai health/condition:

Affecting Factors:

BONSAI TYPE: _____   DATE: _____

PLACING AND POSITIONING

Duration: Visible effect on Bonsai health/condition:

Reactions: Affecting Factors:

WATERING

Frequency:

Visible effect on Bonsai health/condition:

Affecting Factors:

SOIL MIXTURES

Composite:

Estimated quality:

Visible effect/ reactions on Bonsai health/condition:

FERTILIZING

Frequency:

Visible effect on Bonsai health/condition:

Affecting Factors:

BONSAI TYPE: _____   **DATE:** _____

PLACING AND POSITIONING

Duration: Visible effect on Bonsai health/condition:

Reactions: Affecting Factors:

WATERING

Frequency:

Visible effect on Bonsai health/condition:

Affecting Factors:

SOIL MIXTURES

Composite:

Estimated quality:

Visible effect/ reactions on Bonsai health/condition:

FERTILIZING

Frequency:

Visible effect on Bonsai health/condition:

Affecting Factors:

BONSAI TYPE: _____   **DATE:** _____

PLACING AND POSITIONING

Duration: Visible effect on Bonsai health/condition:

Reactions: Affecting Factors:

WATERING

Frequency:

Visible effect on Bonsai health/condition:

Affecting Factors:

SOIL MIXTURES

Composite:

Estimated quality:

Visible effect/ reactions on Bonsai health/condition:

FERTILIZING

Frequency:

Visible effect on Bonsai health/condition:

Affecting Factors:

BONSAI TYPE: _____   **DATE: _____**

PLACING AND POSITIONING

Duration: Visible effect on Bonsai health/condition:

Reactions: Affecting Factors:

WATERING

Frequency:

Visible effect on Bonsai health/condition:

Affecting Factors:

SOIL MIXTURES

Composite:

Estimated quality:

Visible effect/ reactions on Bonsai health/condition:

FERTILIZING

Frequency:

Visible effect on Bonsai health/condition:

Affecting Factors:

BONSAI TYPE: _____ **DATE: _____**

PLACING AND POSITIONING

Duration: Visible effect on Bonsai health/condition:

Reactions: Affecting Factors:

WATERING

Frequency:

Visible effect on Bonsai health/condition:

Affecting Factors:

SOIL MIXTURES

Composite:

Estimated quality:

Visible effect/ reactions on Bonsai health/condition:

FERTILIZING

Frequency:

Visible effect on Bonsai health/condition:

Affecting Factors:

BONSAI TYPE: _____   **DATE:** _____

PLACING AND POSITIONING

Duration: Visible effect on Bonsai health/condition:

Reactions: Affecting Factors:

WATERING

Frequency:

Visible effect on Bonsai health/condition:

Affecting Factors:

SOIL MIXTURES

Composite:

Estimated quality:

Visible effect/ reactions on Bonsai health/condition:

FERTILIZING

Frequency:

Visible effect on Bonsai health/condition:

Affecting Factors:

BONSAI TYPE: _____   **DATE: _____**

PLACING AND POSITIONING

Duration: Visible effect on Bonsai health/condition:

Reactions: Affecting Factors:

WATERING

Frequency:

Visible effect on Bonsai health/condition:

Affecting Factors:

SOIL MIXTURES

Composite:

Estimated quality:

Visible effect/ reactions on Bonsai health/condition:

FERTILIZING

Frequency:

Visible effect on Bonsai health/condition:

Affecting Factors:

BONSAI TYPE: _____   DATE: _____

PLACING AND POSITIONING

Duration: Visible effect on Bonsai health/condition:

Reactions: Affecting Factors:

WATERING

Frequency:

Visible effect on Bonsai health/condition:

Affecting Factors:

SOIL MIXTURES

Composite:

Estimated quality:

Visible effect/ reactions on Bonsai health/condition:

FERTILIZING

Frequency:

Visible effect on Bonsai health/condition:

Affecting Factors:

BONSAI TYPE: _____   **DATE:** _____

PLACING AND POSITIONING

Duration: Visible effect on Bonsai health/condition:

Reactions: Affecting Factors:

WATERING

Frequency:

Visible effect on Bonsai health/condition:

Affecting Factors:

SOIL MIXTURES

Composite:

Estimated quality:

Visible effect/ reactions on Bonsai health/condition:

FERTILIZING

Frequency:

Visible effect on Bonsai health/condition:

Affecting Factors:

BONSAI TYPE: _____   **DATE:** _____

PLACING AND POSITIONING

Duration: Visible effect on Bonsai health/condition:

Reactions: Affecting Factors:

WATERING

Frequency:

Visible effect on Bonsai health/condition:

Affecting Factors:

SOIL MIXTURES

Composite:

Estimated quality:

Visible effect/ reactions on Bonsai health/condition:

FERTILIZING

Frequency:

Visible effect on Bonsai health/condition:

Affecting Factors:

BONSAI TYPE: _____   **DATE:** _____

PLACING AND POSITIONING

Duration: Visible effect on Bonsai health/condition:

Reactions: Affecting Factors:

WATERING

Frequency:

Visible effect on Bonsai health/condition:

Affecting Factors:

SOIL MIXTURES

Composite:

Estimated quality:

Visible effect/ reactions on Bonsai health/condition:

FERTILIZING

Frequency:

Visible effect on Bonsai health/condition:

Affecting Factors:

BONSAI TYPE: _____   **DATE: _____**

PLACING AND POSITIONING

Duration: Visible effect on Bonsai health/condition:

Reactions: Affecting Factors:

WATERING

Frequency:

Visible effect on Bonsai health/condition:

Affecting Factors:

SOIL MIXTURES

Composite:

Estimated quality:

Visible effect/ reactions on Bonsai health/condition:

FERTILIZING

Frequency:

Visible effect on Bonsai health/condition:

Affecting Factors:

BONSAI TYPE: _____   **DATE:** _____

PLACING AND POSITIONING

Duration: Visible effect on Bonsai health/condition:

Reactions: Affecting Factors:

WATERING

Frequency:

Visible effect on Bonsai health/condition:

Affecting Factors:

SOIL MIXTURES

Composite:

Estimated quality:

Visible effect/ reactions on Bonsai health/condition:

FERTILIZING

Frequency:

Visible effect on Bonsai health/condition:

Affecting Factors:

BONSAI TYPE: _____   DATE: _____

PLACING AND POSITIONING

Duration: Visible effect on Bonsai health/condition:

Reactions: Affecting Factors:

WATERING

Frequency:

Visible effect on Bonsai health/condition:

Affecting Factors:

SOIL MIXTURES

Composite:

Estimated quality:

Visible effect/ reactions on Bonsai health/condition:

FERTILIZING

Frequency:

Visible effect on Bonsai health/condition:

Affecting Factors:

BONSAI TYPE: _____   **DATE:** _____

PLACING AND POSITIONING

Duration: Visible effect on Bonsai health/condition:

Reactions: Affecting Factors:

WATERING

Frequency:

Visible effect on Bonsai health/condition:

Affecting Factors:

SOIL MIXTURES

Composite:

Estimated quality:

Visible effect/ reactions on Bonsai health/condition:

FERTILIZING

Frequency:

Visible effect on Bonsai health/condition:

Affecting Factors:

BONSAI TYPE: _____   **DATE:** _____

PLACING AND POSITIONING

Duration: Visible effect on Bonsai health/condition:

Reactions: Affecting Factors:

WATERING

Frequency:

Visible effect on Bonsai health/condition:

Affecting Factors:

SOIL MIXTURES

Composite:

Estimated quality:

Visible effect/ reactions on Bonsai health/condition:

FERTILIZING

Frequency:

Visible effect on Bonsai health/condition:

Affecting Factors:

BONSAI TYPE: _____   **DATE:** _____

PLACING AND POSITIONING

Duration: Visible effect on Bonsai health/condition:

Reactions: Affecting Factors:

WATERING

Frequency:

Visible effect on Bonsai health/condition:

Affecting Factors:

SOIL MIXTURES

Composite:

Estimated quality:

Visible effect/ reactions on Bonsai health/condition:

FERTILIZING

Frequency:

Visible effect on Bonsai health/condition:

Affecting Factors:

BONSAI TYPE: _____   **DATE:** _____

PLACING AND POSITIONING

Duration: Visible effect on Bonsai health/condition:

Reactions: Affecting Factors:

WATERING

Frequency:

Visible effect on Bonsai health/condition:

Affecting Factors:

SOIL MIXTURES

Composite:

Estimated quality:

Visible effect/ reactions on Bonsai health/condition:

FERTILIZING

Frequency:

Visible effect on Bonsai health/condition:

Affecting Factors:

BONSAI TYPE: _____   **DATE:** _____

PLACING AND POSITIONING

Duration: Visible effect on Bonsai health/condition:

Reactions: Affecting Factors:

WATERING

Frequency:

Visible effect on Bonsai health/condition:

Affecting Factors:

SOIL MIXTURES

Composite:

Estimated quality:

Visible effect/ reactions on Bonsai health/condition:

FERTILIZING

Frequency:

Visible effect on Bonsai health/condition:

Affecting Factors:

Printed in Great Britain
by Amazon